unbinding my soul

A Collection of Poetry

CHERYL ROBERTS

Art by Sara Baldwin

unbinding my soul
A Collection of Poetry
Cheryl Roberts

Published by Singular Moments Press, Salt Lake City, UT
Copyright ©2026 Singular Moments Press
All rights reserved.

Project Management and Book Design: DavisCreativePublishing.com
Illustrator/Artist: Sara Baldwin

Publisher's Cataloging-in-Publication
Names: Roberts, Cheryl (Roberts Oliver), author. |
Baldwin, Sara E. (Sara Elsbeth), 1982- illustrator.
Title: Unbinding my soul : a collection of poetry / Cheryl Roberts ; art by Sara Baldwin.
Description: Salt Lake City, UT : Singular Moments Press, [2026]
Identifiers: LCCN: 2025925243 | ISBN: 9798994051504 (paperback) |
9798994051511 (hardback) | 9798994051528 (ebook)
Subjects: LCSH: Liberty. | Self-consciousness (Awareness) | Loss (Psychology) |
Acquiescence (Psychology) | Wisdom. | LCGFT: Poetry. | BISAC: POETRY / Subjects & Themes /
Motivational & Inspirational. | POETRY / General. |
POETRY / Subjects & Themes / Death, Grief, Loss.
Classification: LCC: PS3618.O31562 U53 2026 | DDC: 811/.6--dc233. POE023010
2026

ACKNOWLEDGEMENTS

You know
who you are.

THANK YOU.

TABLE OF CONTENTS

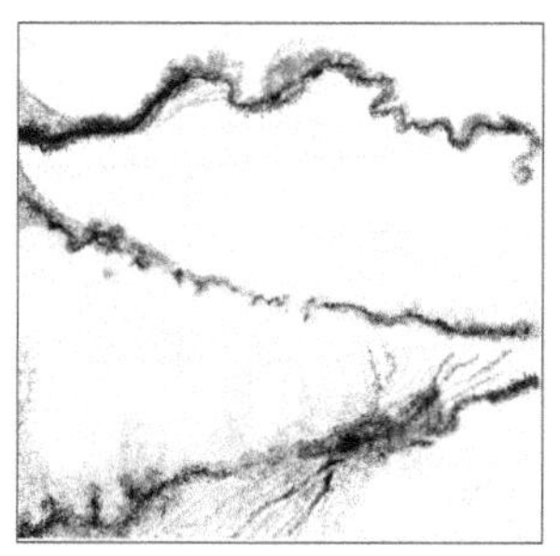

Transformations

Surrendering

Singularities

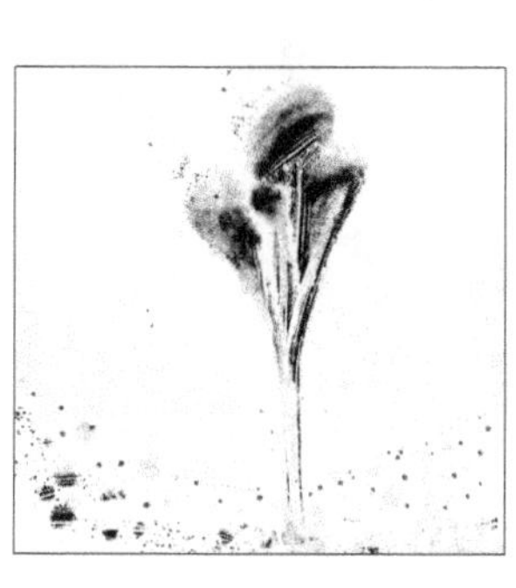

OUR CALLING

Start with Words

Each time you enter an untouched page,
a pristine sheet of real or virtual paper,
acknowledge yourself first
as a single syllable;
then find your noun.

You might feel exposed by
absent adjectives or become
a transitive verb seeking an object.
This exposure, often unintended,
reveals what isn't there, yet.

Perhaps you stumbled
on an unanticipated opening, and, like loose
stones tumbling off canyon walls, there
they are, spilling on the page where they
pause, waiting for delineation.

If you are frightened, you are wise.
Writing is an act of bravery.
The hardest thing is starting.
Then knowing when it's done.

It's all in your mind. You choose.
You decide which words you will
release into the world to fend for
themselves. Then, you start again.

Our Calling

We are called to gather words.
Write, speak, sing, release them
from their silence, revealing
secrets etched into our souls,
every puzzlement and wonder
we feel compelled to disclose.

They cannot be abandoned.
They will wait, each tethered
by the other, yours by mine,
mine by yours, intertwined,
ready to reveal our primal fears,
life's obstructions, our denials.

When too much or too little
tempts us to decline this task,
we need to ask a trusted friend,
an ardent lover, to push us
forward or pull us back into
our purpose.

So let us write, speak, reveal our
stories, poems, songs, exploring
and exposing daily desperations and
ephemeral delights, constantly aware
the sacred thread is made of words
that we are called to share.

The Threads of Time
(A mixed metaphor poem dedicated to Julia Harriet)

We are the seamstresses, weavers
of the threads of time, our spirit fingers
stitching portals into what has been that is no more,
a different place, a different form.
      This life, the last, the next,
        entwined with every breath we take,
        so full, so frail. Death knots the thread.
        Birth spins a new design
formed with sacred colors
of the earth, each dusk and dawn,
reflections of the darkest nights,
always with a flaw to let the spirit out,
        honoring the imperfections
        that overlay the course of growth. Untangling
        the threads, we cast on dreams, a slipknot to begin,
        then we work the yarn of each existence,
entwined with those that came
before and those ahead. We've all been here.
We will return again, traveling a vast expanse
tethered to the now, always seeking to enfold
        and be enfolded in a warm embrace
that will erase our fears and doubts, using
words to calm and comfort when we're lost
only to be found again.
        We are the dreamers,
        rising to new heights, falling to great depths,
        risking loss and pain, knowing that's the price we
         pay for trust and faith to be sustained.
We are the seamstresses,
weavers of the threads, casting on,
working every strand with love, forever
roaming, keepers of unending time.

(First published in The Woman Who Saved Love *by Julia Harriet, 2023)*

A Beginner's Mind

An old soul
enters her earthly form
with a beginner's mind.
Too soon, she slips from
swaddled to smothered
      as layers of limiting beliefs
designed to keep her safe
hold her spellbound, except
      her soul keeps whispering,
            There's so much more,
            so little time. Release
            the threads that bind.
            Gather the divine.

Hidden, always alone,
feeling little and afraid,
      her gifts remained unnamed.
Still, she listened to the desert wind
and stories told by stones and trees,
creatures of all kinds,
breathed poisoned air, and
waited for the end to come. Even then,
      she heard the whispering,
            There's so much more,
            so little time. Release
            the threads that bind.
            Gather the divine.

After decades of unlearning,
and years of gathering the truth,
      the spell unraveled.
At last, at last, she swept her memories
for bits of ancient insight and found
      her beginner's mind,
safely sheltered all these years.
No more whispering,
      she sings aloud,
            There's so much more,
            so little time. Release
            the threads that bind.
            Gather the divine.

Still spry, astute, a sage of sorts, her body
has begun to bend into a crooked line,
      as her mother's did,
and when she holds the staff, those who
know will see her as a guide. The Voice
she hears is loud and clear:
            You are the Crone.
            Now is the time!
            Be the divine.

(First Published in A Beginner's Mind, *a Book of Poetry by Cheryl Roberts with art and images by Sara Baldwin, January 2025)*

Claiming our Stories

In my family, the men did the talking,
telling stories, embellishing, fabricating,

modifying facts to fit their image of themselves,
innately condoning their anger, their blame.

Having outlived them all, I wish I
could share the stories my mother

never told, about how she was
a child when she had her first child,

a sin which bound her to the shadows,
seeking forgiveness that never came.

When asked about her past, she'd say
"It isn't worth remembering," shame

implicit in her voice, her judgment
a reflection of impossible perfection.

Always worried and afraid,
she sealed her pain inside.

Finally, I realize, every line
of every poem I've written,

released not just my own
turmoil and shame,

but hers, because although we
aren't the same, as women,

these are the stories we
must dare to share and claim.

It's All In My Head

I wasn't paralyzed. I could move,
and I did. In circles, never a full stop.

So much thinking, yet I couldn't
hold a simple thought,

relentlessly misusing time,
I dithered, got lost

then heard the
summoning to pause

and listen to my shallow, useless breaths
the rapid beating of my heart.

Achieving nothing, tension
builds, then breaks apart.

I must accept, let fear come
in so I can let it out.

There will be no focused thoughts
today, just random doubt

and circle-spinning angst,
good intentions having fled.

Of course, it is
all in my head.

The Destination

Finally easing my way
out of uncertainty,
seeking comfort,
I unfold
creased maps
with red circles, blue
lines, something to hold,
touch, trace the routes
from there to here,
all those journeys retold
again, and again
moving me away from
or toward, it didn't then
and doesn't matter now,
each choice, every move
from there to here,
still, my maps confirm,
the destination
remains unclear.

All the Interruptions

Each one came
as if it were expected –
pieces of dreams
caught in a heartbeat
abandoned in another,
each one
a distraction
from what had been—
each one,
a view of what's
to come, all the possibilities
caught in a heartbeat
denied in another,
each one
a giving in
of expectations,
never thinking far ahead
or looking far behind
making
an assumption
that uncertainty would
shift and bend, exposing clarity
until one day…
abandoning restraints
it came to us.
With each disruption,
we gained and changed.
We are the interruption.

Shedding

She had no skill
at loving just
a little.

It had been too long,
decades of denial,
of staying safe, so

when she escaped
the refuge walled by
pain and sorrow

by saying yes,
passions long
denied revived.

Amazed, she
knew new choices
must be made.

She would never be
the one she'd been
with others.

She would be the woman
she'd become by
shedding lies and limitations.

SENSUALITY

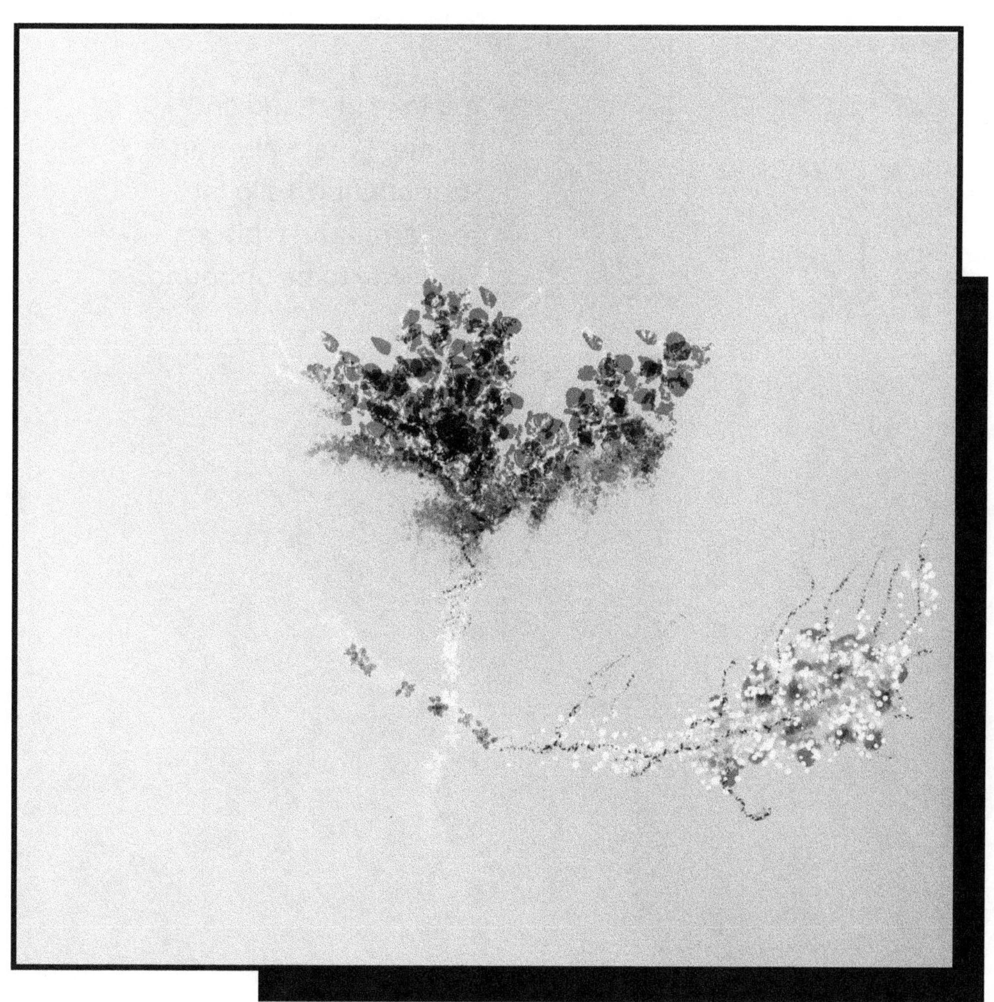

Unbound

It's the Summer Solstice
and I'm giddy with love.
Senses heightened, thoughts
adrift, it feels as if I'm
clinging to the clouds.

I hear a summoning
to touch, to taste.

You take my hand and
ask me, 'What's allowed?'
Surrendering, I slip into
your arms and whisper,
'I'm ready to be unbound.'

Seduction

Tethered by a strand of music
the subtle composition of memories
ephemeral as mist swirling off water
clouds descending, the moon waxing
a touch
       one note
the look
       another note
then the prolonged
exquisite
       tuning of two notes
       into one
the harmony
of bliss-filled convergence
the thread of a memory
caught on a strand of music.

Nascent Love

After days and nights of learning ways
to touch, arouse and satisfy,
absence fills the space we shared.

What brought us to each other?
This friendship formed by
curiosity, our desire to be known.

It was an unhurried awakening.
You were the first to feel more, want more.
I withdrew. You lingered, just out of reach.

Then, I said, "Yes," and the
surrender began. Not submission.
A letting go of all we've known before,

revealing insecurities which, oddly,
fortified our nascent love. For now,
we dwell in words that hold us close,

each hour, redefining patterns.
Sharing stories that reveal our pasts,
we explore embryonic possibilities,

and longing for physical contact,
we linger in articulations
too delicious to disclose.

Sensual

Living up high
the vista is diagonal, oblique,
eye-to-eye with soaring Ravens,
sunlight slanting over shadowed ridges
gathering in transparent cups of
orange and yellow poppy petals
piercing the flesh of red Salvia
on purple stems,
this dusty light that
exposes the sensual drifting of
cottonwood puffs,
other floating things,
before slipping, warm and sultry,
 through an open door.

Still Forming

It begins. It is endless.
We are undefined,
redefined, still forming.
Resistance is futile.
A whole new essence emerges
as we try, fail, start again,
making adjustments
major, minor, each variation
a refinement of content
and technique, as we hone,
carve, shape two separate
lives into possibilities.

Symphony of Spring

As if a conductor were there,
standing in a stiff pose, arms half-raised
indifferent to the chilling rain, the dusting of
powdered snow, a swath of fog,
waiting at the ready for the
Sun's opening glance.
Then, an imperceptible
flick of the baton and the first notes
begin to fill the air, a lively allegro
heralding warmth as sunlight spills
down the mountain, a gentle adagio
releasing the scent of cedar,
sage and pine, grasses stretching
poco a poco, scrub oaks leafing in largo,
then allargando as the music slows, grows
louder, culminating in a
chorus of Corvidae
calling up the day!

As the Morning Stirs

As rays of sunlight fall
on still-closed eyes,
I abandon dreams
(such as they were)
in a vain attempt to catch
every word spilling
into consciousness,
my reservoir of sleep
flooded with inane,
luminous, escaping
thoughts that,
out of context,
lose all meaning
as the morning stirs.

Liminal Boundary

Eyelids lifting
in time to see
layers of color
behind unleafed
willow branches
and a motionless
pond reflecting
the same steel gray
as the sky,
a liminal boundary
between the
edge of night and
the first glimmer
of light.

Dance of the Willows

        At rest, they appear
to be a tangled sort of tree, with
sinewy limbs and feathery leaves,
growing wild along the highway
with sage-green Russian Olives, or
here, between the fence and the shed.
        Then comes a puff of wind
and their dance begins, swaying,
swishing long, thin leaves
entwining with each other,
pale gray exposed on one side,
lime on the other,
        being caressed by
rather than submitting to the wind
that may be blowing south-south-east
or north-westerly, the golden willow limbs
move back and forth, indifferent to
direction or intention,
        as if just threading
leaves and dancing in the breeze
fulfilled their only purpose.

The Subtle Shifts of Time

      Almost invisible,
nearly imperceptible, the movement
of the earth, the shifting of our lives.
      Daylight arrived a minute
later this morning, and will depart too
soon this afternoon.
      For years, I measured
time by the lengthening of
shadows spilling, long and lean,
      across an urban park.
Now I watch an ever-changing
moon rise over a mountain,
      inches away from
where it came up yesterday.
All so subtle, so singular,
      reminders to be aware,
observant, patient. With so much
churning, rushing to survive, the
      Winter Solstice arrives
Just in time to call to mind,
right now, this moment,
      we can pause
and rest, find magic, create
sacred space, and use this dark season
      to align our lives
with what we want the most,
becoming the best that we can be.

UNCERTAINTY

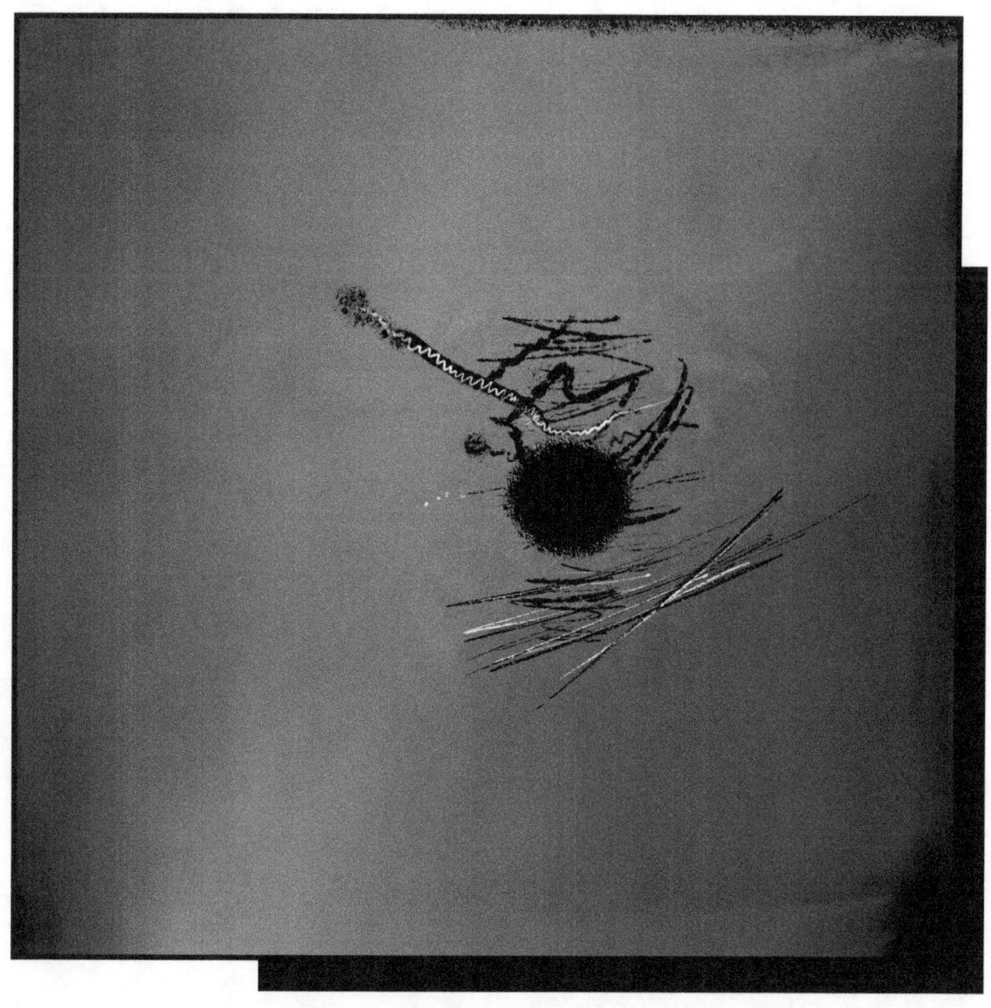

The Ending

It seemed important. Even urgent.
Powerful enough to dissolve a vow,
erode a bond, dismantle hope,
deconstruct a life.

Sitting in this moment, just before sunrise,
watching time stretch into a thin line,
that oh-so-important shift is revealed in
its most subtle forms:

> trust evaporating;
> an involuntary altercation;
> the withdrawal of affection.

The ending came because
nothing sustainable remained.

Still Here

       I'm still here,
inside this body with its faulty thermostat,
crepey skin, thinning bones and thoughts that
drift away, unformed.
       I know we both see
       how lost I feel at times.
       And yet, last Mother's Day
we laughed, gardened, played together,
and in four more days, we will celebrate
the anniversary of your birth.
       I'm ill-prepared, just as
       I was when emergency surgery
       saved our lives.
How did we do it, the two of us, learning as
we went, making mistakes. adjusting, revising,
seeking better strategies?
       Still, I'm here,
inside this vessel that fills and spills
as spontaneously as the thunderstorm
we had this morning.
       Still self-absorbed,
       frail, I'm a bit afraid
       of what I cannot do,
words I won't be able to unearth,
thoughts I cannot catch and hold.
Nothing too intense, yet.

       For now, I'll focus on
       your birthday.
       You've put your
foot down. You're not planning
your own party, making your own cake,
decorating the space.
       That's what
       I will do, since
       I'm still here, inside
this body that birthed you,
that, at times, gets fatigued
from wounds inflicted by
       inadequacy.
       I'm supposed
       to be brave.
I am brave. Still here
I will make a cake, decorate.
Still, until the end of time,
       your mother.
       rooted in
       gratitude.

So Little Time

a baby's fist, fingers folded,
only opening to clutch another

my mother, eyes closed,
grasps my hand and gasps for air

my oldest brother
gone with no goodbye; too late, I realize.

fingers clutching,
a last gasp, another brother dies

we have so little time
between our first breath, our last regret.

Transient

The earth does not clutch at the sky.
It breaks, layer on layer exposing
the eras it survived, revived from.
     We, teetering on this
transient threshold, are brief
inhabitants, balanced on a narrow
ledge of destruction and discovery.
     Adorned with technologies
designed for their own survival,
we fail to honor narratives revealed
by glacier- and water-carved
     canyons, by fossils exposed
in strata eroded by fire and ice,
wind and water. Is it any wonder
we can't contemplate what
     the layers will reveal
     when we're extinct?

Shielding

Part I

Even if it isn't
said out loud, we still
wonder how much
pain will be involved in the
next transformation,

this shift into a place
we've never been, where
memories are erased
and wisdom must be regained.

First, our bodies grew,
bones lengthened,
no more baby teeth,
hands and feet got bigger,
no more cuddling.

To have grown
is to have lost and gained,
and yes, we felt the pain.
Not just the changing
structure of our bodies,

but the need to shield
emerging, eager spirits.
Before we learned
the words that could explain,
we connected lines

we spelled our names,
we sheltered in our fears
and then the bigger changes
came, thoughts and feelings,
the awful shame that,
without our knowing,
wasn't ours to own.

Part II

It's late now. Our
grown-up anger erased that
unnamed shame.
At this stage, we've more
important things

to contemplate.
Shrinking, brittle bones,
weathered skin,
things we lose, then find again,

memories wrapped
in cellophane.

Each adjustment made
to ease an ache or
lessen stress and strain,
seems temporary.
We hold a new shame
that isn't ours. It's just that
we are growing old

and in our frailty,
we're afraid to ask for help
or have it seem
as if we cannot make it
on our own.

And so we linger in
uncertainty, still shielding
lost souls
and secrets we told
ourselves to
help us stay alive.

Part III
      Another myth
exposed as fallacy, once
      unshielded, erases
who or what we thought
      should be protected.

Now we know, we
      are fully aware that
this singular moment in time
      is all we have
What a relief.
      What a waste to use
what little we have left
      dwelling in doubts.

      Let's not dither
our days away, caught in what
      the Buddhists say
are hindrances. It's time
      to be released from
worries; time to claim
      the freedom
we have earned to leap
      headfirst, heart forward
unshielded, unrestrained
      to flex our aging parts,
and, as if anew, send our
      eager spirits out to play.

The List of Losses

My alarm died. I am able to sleep
uninterrupted. I still wake at 3 a.m.,
the time when I gave her the insulin
shot she needed to function.
Now, I remain quiet when I wake,
listening to the dark, to the moaning of the
night that holds so many secrets, the myths
that remind me I am just another creature
wandering the earth in a dreamless state,
waiting…for what…for my mournful heart
to thump me out of sleep, alert me that time
is being lost. Losing time, losing dreams, losing
hope… it's such a long list, and yes, I know the
list of what I've found and what I'm yet to find
is even longer, but right now, in this moment,
I've given up on holding fast, and in
my letting go, must recognize and redefine

what brings delight so I might finally forsake fear.

TRANSFORMATIONS

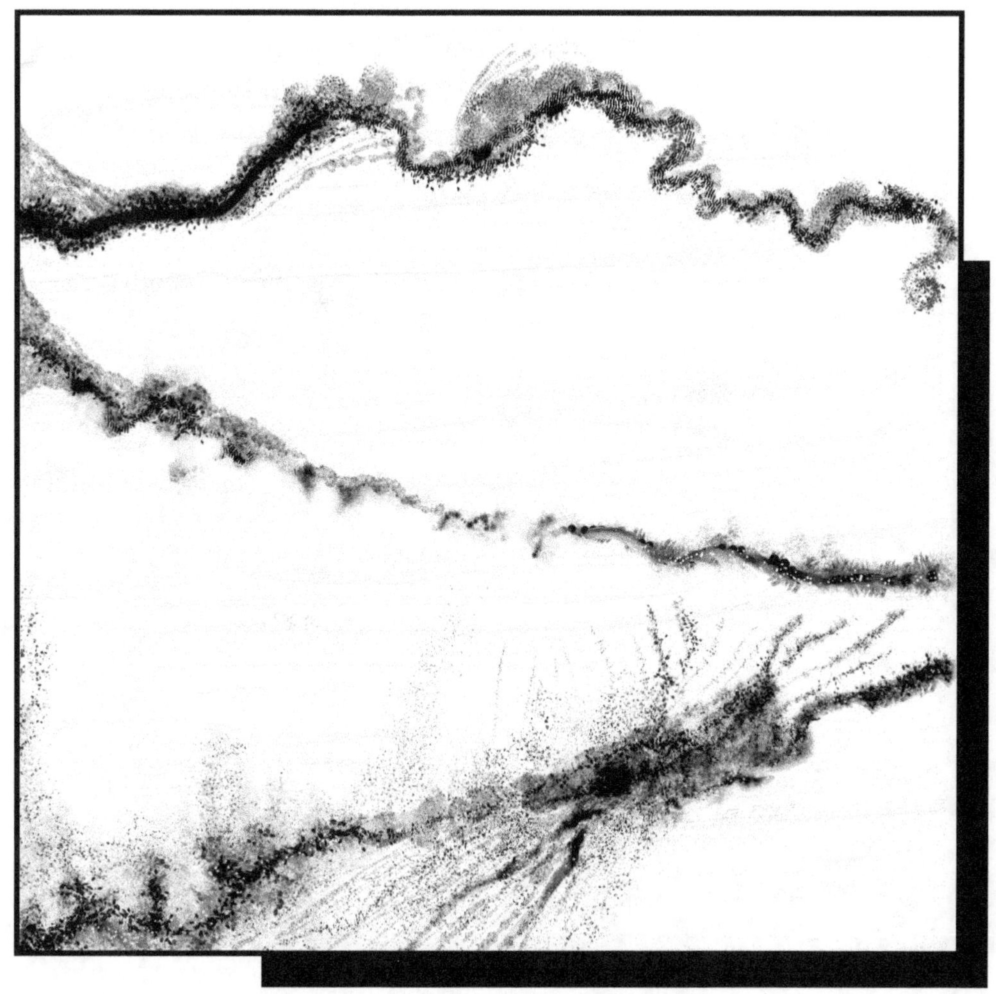

Enchantments

Enchantments abound,
surround and infuse,
as subtle as the
crusted edge
that lichen carves on stone,
as silent as crumpled
poppy petals pushing
aside a brown husk
before unfurling in
the morning sun.

She Decides

A child pretends, blends, observes,
learns everyone is angry or afraid.
Wishing to be unseen, she decides

to hide her real self. It's easy.
Battered by momentum,
no one really sees her, so she decides

motion will be added to her disguise,
reasoning, if she's always on her way,
no one will know if she never arrives.

Then one day, she wondered if her real self,
the one that she'd been keeping safe,
had been misplaced.

So long ignored, denied, deprived,
she decides it's time to excavate
her sacred bits and pieces.

She shivered as she realized who she
might have been will never be.
She decides, "Just as well, it's for the best."

Now she can be the woman she's
become, this imperfect one,
she's finally learned to trust and love.

(First published as 'Just as Well' in Shift With Intention and Soar,
compiled by Jaime Zografos, 2022)

The Chaos of an Unconscious Mind

Uncountable
unsortable, a mangle of
words, images clamoring
demanding immediate attention
the repetitive notes of an annoying tune
names not quite remembered
all pushing and shoving,
crowded in a space with no dimension
caught in a singular span of time
before limbs
stiff from all-night poses stretch
and pressure shifts off aching
shoulders, knees, hips
just
before
the eyelids lift
then it's all so swift, chaos swept away
relegated to the dark
unfinished realm, waiting to be sorted
organized and gathered into
calm, clear, actionable thoughts—
It's good to be awake.

(First published in Clarity Out Of Chaos, *an anthology
compiled by Cathy L. Davis, 2021)*

Break of Day

Let's linger a little longer,
here, in the almost light, with thoughts that do not nag
and dreams that form and reform, emerging at the break of day.
This dawn, dark clouds
hover in the north and south, along the east horizon, erasing
the edge between earth and sky, a reminder that opposites
need not be in opposition
and that, in fact, we need the friction
of differences.
Difficulty is our
master teacher, the one who makes us
name our discontent, teaching
us to face our fears.
Which is why we hold so dear these undemanding
moments when mindless movements
guide us into mindfulness.
Let's linger here a little longer, delaying decisions,
evading actions, abiding in this sacred space we're gifted with
each break of day.

There is a Lingering

After wind and rain bare-limbed
even Cottonwood trees,
expectations litter the path.

The air is still. Hazy sunlight
cannot warm this bone-deep
cold or ease an anxious
lingering that stretches
long and thin on this late
end-of-autumn afternoon.

Just before nightfall,
hearing a whisper,
we pause and move aside,
able at last to let
our troubled pasts, no
longer offering refuge,
scurry on by.

Essential Repairs

When the moving parts
start to stop, when thoughts
scatter and vision dims, it is time
to schedule repairs. But first we
must be prepared to answer,
"What needs fixing?"
    What, in our last life, did
we jury-rig that this time 'round
required all new underpinnings?
Not just unresolved beginnings.
It's those unsettled endings that
ripple through time.
    We're all broken,
imperfect, doused with failure,
awash with unmet expectations.
It is a wonder we keep trying.
But we do, each time going
deeper into the shadows
    to be reminded,
"We can't go on like this."
We can no longer pretend or
justify making the same errors
over and over and over again.
Is it just perpetuation,
    the repetition
of being born, evolving, adept and
smart, before we start to tear
apart? The spirits are not malicious.

They place debris in our path,
prompting us to focus on awareness,
    on acceptance,
on being willing to begin again.
We've mended wounds, our own
and others, knowing each repair revealed
what got us here, and why
it wasn't quite enough.
    Next time,
although wiser and stronger,
our essence remains unstable, still
disabled by makeshift habits and
behaviors unbound and rebound
with 12-step bailing wire
    that, though helpful,
were not enough. It's true, we're
making progress, each iteration
guiding us toward a better way.
We wait with equal longing
and reluctance for this one
    to end and the next
to begin, almost new, with
fewer shadows, more delight,
insight, and acceptance. Repairs
are essential. Becoming
takes many lifetimes.

It Matters

> For decades,
> she was sand washed by waves,
> a stone rolled to smoothness
>   by the river;
> a cumulus cloud pushed by
> winds circling this
>   trembling sphere,
> a seed, resting on the surface,
> rootless, stemless.
>   Then she named
> her gift, and words began
> to form her purpose.
>   Now she grows
> clearer with each transformation,
> lighter with each abandonment
>   of limitations,
> letting go of a life, two-thirds over,
> to better embrace the final third,
>   by being honest
> with herself, then with others,
> knowing that, even when it doesn't seem
>   to matter,
>   it always matters.

Immersion

A leaf released from its limb
glides onto the surface of a pool,
edges softening, affirming
the simplicity of dissolution
as it is immersed in the
murky, nutrient-rich
pond, to be absorbed.

      We can't know
such freedom. It is not our nature.
We cling, even past our natural
time, holding fast as our surfaces
change tones and textures.

Is death an immersion?
Is it the not knowing that keeps
us fastened to this form?

Uncertain of what we become
when we unbecome, we keep
breathing, clinging, choosing
one more sliver of joy before
our edges soften, before our
immersion in otherness.

Unbecoming

I will enter the doorway that is my body,
I will slow my pace, feel my grace, and listen.
Is it essential to listen…deeply.

On the outside, cells are dying.
They sing of their demise.

Inside, vulnerable emotions
risk exposure with their voices.
It is essential to listen…deeply.

Canceling the inner and the outer noise,
I mold a space made only of vibrations,

a singing bowl, chimes with echoing tones
resonate within my brittle bones.
It is essential to listen…deeply.

(From the Warrior Series)

Tumbleweed

Another windy day,
and I, mature and dry,
prepare to detach,
so that I may smoothly
bounce and tumble
across four states,

intending to deposit
seeds of compassion
and kindness along the way,
setting positive intentions,
my survival mantra for
these troubled days.

When I landed in the
Midwest thirty years ago,
I was a rolling, rootless weed
snagged instantly by expectations
that, though never realized,
somehow morphed into a life.

Now it's time to return
to my original roots and
the high-mountain deserts
that shaped my underlying
limitations…a hard edge
and reluctance to trust.

My departure will be,
as was my arrival,
in the hot and humid
thick of summer.
Like the tumbleweed,
I take only what I need.

SURRENDERING

At Last

At last,
listening to the
insistent affirmation
of my soul, I consent
to feelings long denied,
and yielding,
name it strength.
At last,
listening to
the lulling voice
of empathy, I sense
each hairline fracture
in the shell I formed,
and breaking,
name it strength.
At last,
listening to
the whisper of
hope, love welcomes
the wholeness of this
fragile human heart,
and weeping,
names it strength.

All That Remains

One more step
into that irksome unknown
that taunts and tempts
      don't risk it
      don't miss this chance
just one step, one decision
once made alters all that
follows, as the plague of
"what ifs" crawl inside
      you can, you can't
      you will, you won't
lifting the foot, putting it down
pulling it back
      too risky, too old
      too comfortable
you know what you
know so well. Your routine
is safe, and yet,
if you don't take
it while you can,
that one last chance
to overcome, become
you'll find
      too soon
is not an option.
You've only got
      before it's too late.
This is the step you have to take
to be fully alive for
all that remains.

(First published in Here Comes the Sun, *an anthology
compiled by Mistilei Wriston, 2022)*

The Algorithm

When does it start?
The diminishing, the un-becoming,
tumbling into mediocrity,
fitting in, growing ever less aware
of being crushed by innuendo, discord,
light and dark smeared into gray,
dullness, numbness hunkered in to stay.

And then, in our maturity,
having grown certain only of uncertainty,
we keep doing what we've always done.
That's the safest way, denying any
thought or deed that might reveal
our facile resignation, each abdication that,
let's not forget, we still embrace.

What was formed to
keep us safe now suckles us with
residue and repetition. Our unconscious
state assimilates and replicates
every habit and addiction, offering
comfort as our consolation. When
did we become the algorithm?

Odds N' Ends and Bits of Sorrow

        Saved until last,
assuming it won't take long to sort and box
the final odds and ends, but then, the contents
seem to say, *let me stay in this little drawer
you rarely open. There are reasons you've
forgotten what you kept in here.*
        Way in the back,
snuggled into corners, you find feelings
unexpressed, kept from view, held in a book of
matches from The Barbizon, and farther back,
the pewter ashtray marked by memories of times
when cigarettes and sex were satisfying.
        You thought sorting
these long-forgotten items would be simple,
but discover instead, these kept things
must be safely packed and taken with you
to another place reserved for odd n' ends
of satisfaction, bits of sorrow, unforgotten.

Surrendering

        Thawing, like freezing
but more visible, happens in layers,
slowly as crystals melt, or suddenly
as clumps of snow collapse
off pine boughs. It can also be
disguised, subtle as black ice,
        or symbolic, as
we recognize it's time to shed the fears
we used to stay alive. It will be hard.
If only we, like sycamores, could let our
withered bark peel off to gently bare
abandoned dreams,
that still as death, somehow survived.
        Lying in wait, an
impatient ego lures us with
the swooning, slumping
threat of fresh abandonment,
a tempting ploy to keep us
trapped inside our paradox.
        We hear our inner
voices, the ones that always caution us
to wait, but bolstered by awareness,
we detach ourselves from pain
that has become irrelevant, which
is a process, a project that has commenced
        again and again,
each stage silenced by our first companions –
fear and doubt – formed to keep our little
selves and secrets safe. Now, we silence them.

You see, we've learned surrendering is
not the same as giving up or giving in.
        It is assenting
to the deferred demise of useless attitudes
and vain conceits, a rebuttal
to the acts of insolence, a leaving off of
habits and addictions that will no longer
keep us from emerging, as we thaw.

(First published in Resilience, *an anthology
compiled by Jennifer Bardot, 2023)*

Each Time the First and Only

       Ancient wisdom
courses through our veins,
the genius of survival,
the virtuosity of transformation,
lessons learned on battlegrounds,
in fields of lavender,
at firepits and hearths,
in barns and trenches,
lingering at deathbeds,
rocking tiny cradles.
       Our souls enfold the
mysteries and misdeeds we need
to reconcile, the blessings of
kindness, loves we were denied,
loves that thrived. Each time we left
so much behind, choosing to
become another, to be born in
innocence, swaddled
        in vulnerability,
knowing all we cherished,
all that broke our spirits
and our hearts would be erased,
that all we learned would
be forgotten, making
each and every time the first
and only life. What courage!
We are brave indeed.

(First Published in A Beginner's Mind, *a Book of Poetry by
Cheryl Roberts with art and images by Sara Baldwin, January 2025)*

No Going Back

decisively
irreversibly
beyond any doubt
there's no going back
        but then
resistance starts
        the urge to fix what feels
unfinished, to re-sort
        what was packed
in boxes, moved from
place-to-place,
stored in closets,
        just in case.

        Instead,
with age, uncertainty prevails
and we debate which doubts to trust
        the most, which the least,
using questions to distract, displace
until one day it's clear.
        There's no going back,
it can't be fixed, and most of
what was packed can, at last,
        be tossed away.

Trying to re-open the portal to my barely found soul.

I'm there. On the
other side. Again.
Darker than last time,
different, not a sliver of light,
just dim shadows.

There! Just then, I felt
the pull of my mother's
strength that I called weakness.

She draws me out,
admonishing,
        "This isn't someone
        else's map."

I keep circling
finding a few signposts
        essential in a
        directionless life.

All the times I've gotten lost,
I pretended to be found. Now,
If I don't look back
if I look ahead
if I'm finally honest
Will I arrive?
How will I know?
        I'll need
more signposts.

I'm here.
Intent on unbinding my soul.
It was pure this time,
barely formed, unviolated.

Instead, I find the hairline crack
where shame spilled
into me.

Be wary, she whispers.
"Quickly,
        mend the
        crack."

I keep repeating, I can't
keep doing this.
        This is the last
        time.

With much less time
ahead than what has
come before,
if I am lucky,
if I say yes
if I say no
if I hold love close,
        can I reopen the
portal to my barely
found soul?

The First Assumption

The day begins with
an assumption
that we will be
able to slide our legs
from under the sheet,
place them over
the edge of the bed,
plant our feet and stand,
even with pain,
then one foot at a time,
seeking balance,
we step into a day filled
with innumerable
assumptions.

What I've learned this year…

(Election Year 2024)
…hope can be crushed…life goes on.
…too little, too late… the curse of delay.
…thinking ahead…lost in space
      for an hour, sometimes days.
      Imaginations fray, as if only
      holes hold scraps in place.

Lived experiences remain. Grasping
onto long ago seems crystal clear, until
whatever thought we caught a moment
      before, just slips away,
      a word misplaced,
      a motion mystified.

Then grief settles in, as if it were invited.
It promises not to be too needy
or too troubling, but it is both.
      It cannot help itself.
      It will not be ignored.
      We know. We've tried.

And so, we face reality. This year will end.
The next four will begin. Some feel fear,
others rejoice, differences keep us apart.
      What remains? A force, an
      energy that builds, shifts,
      moving with a bifurcated purpose.

SINGULARITIES

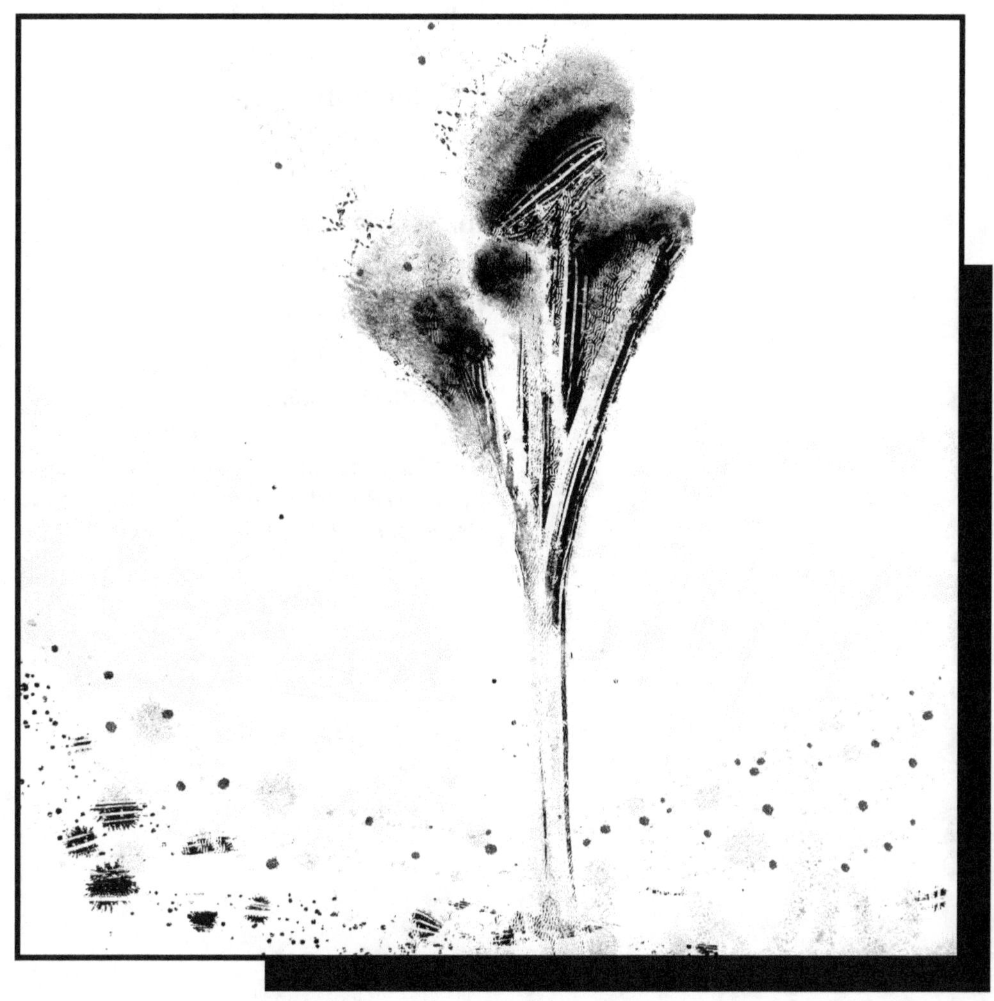

A Puff

Late evening on the balcony
after a cooling rain,
celebrating equal hours of day and night,
five hummingbirds came to play
sipping Lavendar and Golden Fennel flowers
resting on the trellis.
One flies up to me,
hovers briefly, eye to eye
then, without a whisper
they are gone
leaving a puff…
that's what sailors call it…
that pulse of air that
comes out of nowhere,
this one stirred
to life by shimmering
emerald wings.

(First Published in The Season Journal, *a Book of Poetry by Cheryl Roberts with art and images by Sara Baldwin, December 2021)*

The Dying Time

Sprawling mounds of burnt orange
and sepia blend with blue-gray and ochre
on foothills refreshed by cold rain, while
high on mountain peaks, the first snow
of the season glistens
      in light that only shines this clearly
      when the air itself can breathe.
This is a dying time, a pause,
when restlessness becomes a
passage to stillness. Another
ending, a shifting of energy.
Rather than engaging in urgent
      festivities intended to rebuff
      whatever awaits us in
the long darkness ahead,
let's immerse our souls in the
slow dance of change, and, like deep
roots and fattening bulbs, cultivate
awareness for our spring emergence.

ESE at Three Miles Per Hour

A wispy little thing
flowing east-southeast
across the oaks and sycamores
through the open balcony door
delivering the scent of drying leaves
bursting Goldenrods, the spice
of prairie grasses ripe with seeds
and just a trace of evening rain.

(First Published in The Season Journal, *a Book of Poetry
by Cheryl Roberts with art and images by Sara Baldwin,
December 2021)*

Sending Love on a Whisper of Air

This morning, before sunrise, I watched
snowflakes drift down, swirl around, float away.
Every living thing was cloaked in silence, detained
in the space between whispers of air.
Instead of rushing in or dashing off, I listened to
the silence. Crystals formed on skin and hair,
spirits soared, my form was not the same. Finally
snagged by the currents of time, I journeyed to a place
I rarely dare to go, the place inside where feelings hide. Sur-
rendering to hope, I unwrapped gratitude, counted blessings,
then, tenderly unwound the bindings from my heart.
Memories linger in this space where nothing
needs doing, this crescent of time when
emotions wander unrestrained, flowing in
and out, recalling all that came before,
accepting what is here and now, believing
in the yet to be. I released a silent prayer, aware,
knowing that even though we're far apart, my love
would drift to you on a whisper of air.

After the Winter Solstice

       Now it begins, our arduous climb
out of the dark, watching for any
hint of added light, seconds only,
minutes, almost measurable,
if not to our eyes, at least to our spirits,
a persistent reminder to be patient.
       Planets align, the universe shifts,
our lives are not the same. It's time,
again, to unbind whatever
holds our hope in shackles, time to
revive our expectations, believe in something –
most of all ourselves!
       Here's to letting go of holding back,
to searching high and low for every
little joy, to nourishing starved souls
with laughter, and by listening,
hear the voice that lures us onward
to adventure and renewal.

(First Published in The Season Journal, *a Book of Poetry
by Cheryl Roberts with art and images by Sara Baldwin,
December 2021)*

On This Longest Day

…let your senses soar
and thoughts drift
silent as the clouds
        release
        resistance,
        be undone
perceive every texture,
receive every sound,
savor each flavor
        breathe in
        hold on
        let go
renew your
sense of wonder
become the other
        you've been
        waiting for,
        satisfy
longings, surrender
to change, on this
        the
        longest
        day.

ABOUT THE AUTHOR

When she retired in 2018, Cheryl Roberts decided to sneak in one more lifelong dream. She became an independent writing coach and editor with Davis Creative Publishing.

After returning to her roots in the West in 2022, she shifted her focus to her poetry, coaching, and facilitating online writing workshops for aspiring authors ready to get started or unstuck.

She can be reached through FACEBOOK: Cheryl.oliver.948

ABOUT THE ARTIST

Sara Baldwin | Inspired Art

Sara has always been inspired by wild places and wild things. Her art captures the vivid colors and textures found in nature. She works with acrylic and oil paints, digital mediums, and photography. She is a Salt Lake City native and loves Utah's wild places.

You can find her on Instagram
@sarabaldwin_inspiredart

Artist website:
https://3-sara-baldwin.pixels.com

NOTE:
Cheryl and Sara are mother and daughter and love spending time together, exploring and being silly. This is their third collaborative poetry and art book.